CORAL REEFS

THE SEA

Jason Cooper

The Rourke Corporation, Inc.
Vero Beach, Florida 32964

Edited by Sandra A. Robinson

PHOTO CREDITS
All photos © Mary A. Cote except page 8, © Margarette Mead

LIBRARY OF CONGRESS
Library of Congress Cataloging-in-Publication Data
Cooper, Jason, 1942-
    Coral reefs / by Jason Cooper.
    p. cm. — (Discovery library of the sea)
    Includes index.
    Summary: Describes the animals known as corals, the formation of
the reefs they build, and life in this unique habitat.
    ISBN 0-86593-229-8
    1. Coral reef fauna—Juvenile literature. 2. Coral reef ecology—
Juvenile literature. 3. Coral reefs and islands—Juvenile literature.
[1. Corals. 2. Coral reef ecology. 3. Ecology.] I. Title. II. Series:
Cooper, Jason, 1942-   Discovery library of the sea.
QL125.C66 1992
591.9'1—dc20   92-16077
                                                    CIP
                                                    AC

Printed in the USA

TABLE OF CONTENTS

CORAL REEFS

One of nature's most remarkable **habitats,** or homes, for sea life is the coral reef.

A coral reef is a formation of limestone rock made by coral animals under the sea.

When coral animals die, their "skeletons," made of rock-hard limestone, remain. Living corals continue to make limestone, and the reef continues to grow.

Coral formation on a reef in the Caribbean Sea

REEFS AROUND THE WORLD

The kinds, or **species,** of corals that build reefs live only in ocean water that is warm, clear and shallow. Along the coasts of the mainland United States, only southern Florida has living coral reefs. One of the best is at John Pennekamp Coral Reef State Park in Key Largo. Boats take visitors to the reef, about five miles offshore.

One of Australia's greatest attractions is the Great Barrier Reef. This coral reef follows the Australian coast for about 1,250 miles.

Brain coral (bottom) and blue chromis fish thrive on a living Caribbean reef

CORAL ANIMALS

All coral animals are soft and delicate, like their jellyfish cousins. Corals that build the rock-hard reefs are known as "hard" corals. "Soft" corals build beautiful fanlike and whiplike structures that sway in ocean currents.

The coral animal itself, called a polyp, is a fleshy little tube. It has lacy "fingers," or **tentacles,** around its mouth.

Some coral species are found in cold water, but none of them builds reefs.

Lacy sea fan is one of the "soft" corals

THE GROWING REEF

Each "hard" coral polyp poduces limestone to form its "skeleton"—the cuplike structure in which it lives. Like concrete, the limestone begins as a liquid, then hardens to rock.

Reef-building corals live in **colonies,** or groups. Each polyp, beneath its cup, is connected to the next polyp.

When polyps die, living corals build onto their limestone "skeletons." After many years, the growing mass of limestone may become a large reef or even a coral island.

Colony of "hard" coral polyps feeding at night

Flower coral, one of the reef-builders, during the day

Flower coral polyps emerge at night to feed

THE COLORFUL CORALS

A coral reef is a lively world of color and unusual beauty. Rainbow-colored sea creatures of every description live on the reef. Coral formations themselves may be tan, green, orange, purple or a number of other colors.

Corals grow in many curious shapes, many of them revealed by names such as brain, staghorn, boulder, finger, flower, cactus, elkhorn and pillar.

*Sponges nearly cover a
coral rock "tower"*

LIFE ON THE CORAL REEF

The coral reef is a community of saltwater, or **marine,** plants and animals. All of the **organisms**— the living things—in the community are important to each other.

Predators (the hunters) and **prey** (the hunted) live on the coral reef. Sometimes the hunter becomes the hunted. Coral polyps prey at night on tiny animals that drift into their tentacles. In turn, corals are food for certain sea urchins, fish, worms and sponges.

Queen angelfish resting among corals (top) and a sponge (bottom)

ANIMALS OF THE REEF

A living coral reef looks like a rock garden of strange, brightly-colored plants. But the "rocks" are living coral formations and most of the "plants" are animals—sea feathers, sponges, anemones, sea lilies, sea urchins, fan-worms and others. Many of these animals, like plants, are fixed to one location.

Some of the reef animals, of course, swim or crawl. Among them are fish, crabs, lobsters, starfish, jellyfish, sea slugs and snails.

Banded shrimp pauses on a dark volcano sponge on a Caribbean coral reef

EXPLORING A CORAL REEF

The best way to explore the wonders of a coral reef is to become a fish. But the next best way is to put on snorkel or scuba gear.

Snorkelers swim on the surface of the water and look down at the reef through a watertight mask. They breathe air through a tube called a snorkel.

Scuba divers carry air tanks from which they breathe. Scuba divers can plunge down to the reef and explore its tiny mountains and canyons.

Scuba diver swims toward tube sponge growing from coral formation

PROTECTING CORAL REEFS

Living coral reefs are like fine glass—beautiful, but easily destroyed.

Corals need clean, clear water in which to live. Human activities that add dirt and poisons to the water can easily destroy coral reefs.

Coral reefs in Florida and the Caribbean Sea are also threatened by coral collectors. Coral rock is sold as souvenirs and for use in aquariums.

Glossary

colonies (KAHL uh neez) — a group of animals of the same kind living together

habitat (HAB uh tat) — the kind of place in which an animal lives, such as a coral reef

marine (muh REEN) — of or relating to the sea, salt water

organism (OR gan izm) — a living thing

predator (PRED uh tor) — an animal that kills other animals for food

prey (PRAY) — an animal that is hunted by another for food

scuba diver (SKOO ba DI ver) — one who swims under water with the help of special breathing equipment (air tanks)

snorkeler (SNOR kel er) — one who swims with the help of a special breathing tube (snorkel)

species (SPEE sheez) — within a group of closely related animals, such as corals, one certain kind or type (*brain* coral)

tentacles (TEN tah kulz) — a group of long, flexible body parts usually growing around an animal's mouth and used for touching, grasping or stinging

INDEX